T0085997

Pre-reader

Sleep, Bear!

Shelby Alinsky

NATIONAL
GEOGRAPHIC

Washington, D.C.

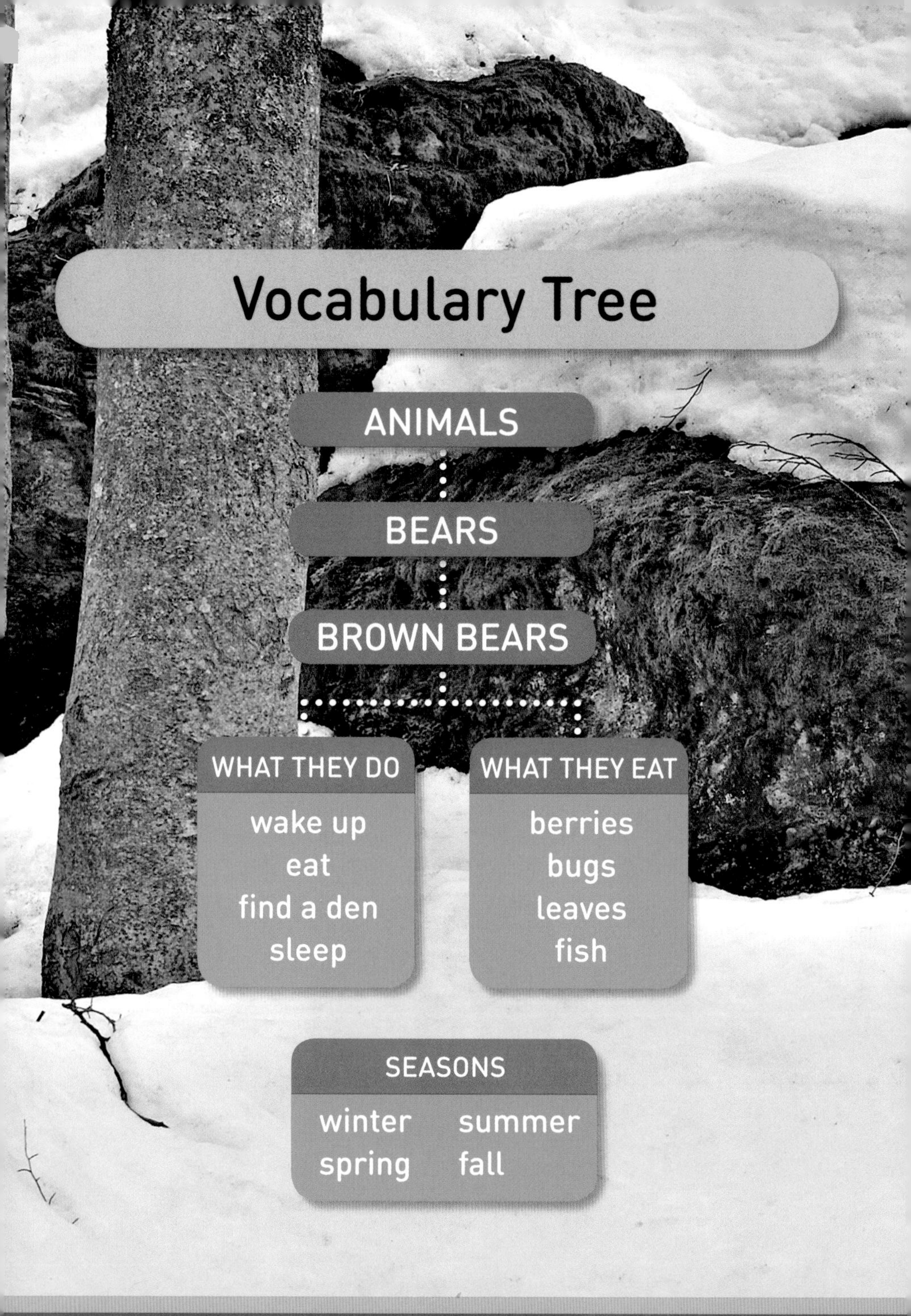

Vocabulary Tree

ANIMALS

BEARS

BROWN BEARS

WHAT THEY DO

wake up
eat
find a den
sleep

WHAT THEY EAT

berries
bugs
leaves
fish

SEASONS

winter   summer
spring   fall

Winter is over. Wake up, bear!

It's spring. The days are cool.

The bear is hungry.
It hasn't eaten all winter.

Bugs are good, too.

So is grass.

Now the days are getting warm.

The sun shines. It's summer.

In summer, the bear eats
lots of bugs.

There is also something special

for the bear to eat.

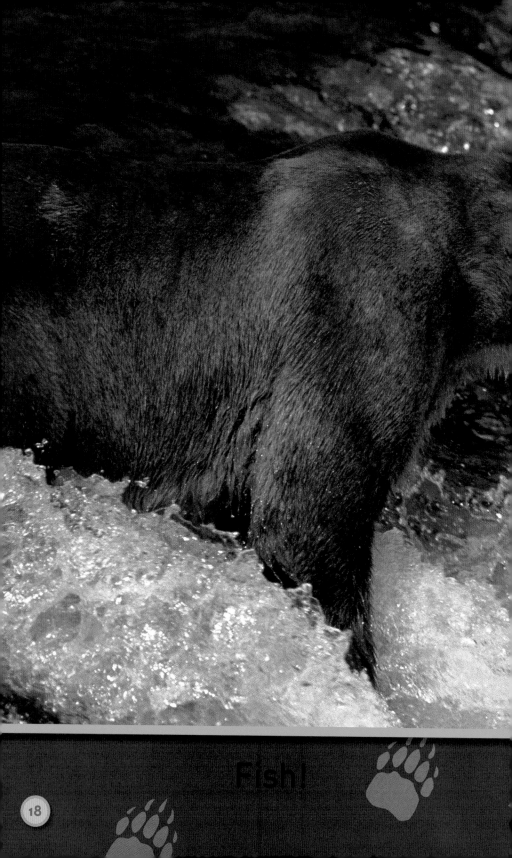

Fish!

Now the days are getting cool.

It's fall. The bear finds a den.

Sleep, bear!

YOUR TURN!

Be a brown bear!
Act out what the bear does
in each season.

WHAT DOES THE BEAR DO IN SPRING?

WHAT DOES THE BEAR DO IN SUMMER?

WHAT DOES THE BEAR DO IN FALL?

WHAT DOES THE BEAR DO IN WINTER?

The publisher gratefully acknowledges the expert content review of this book by Jason Matthews, master naturalist, Montana Natural History Center/Montana Outdoor Science School, and the expert literacy review by Susan B. Neuman, Ph.D., professor of Early Childhood and Literacy Education, New York University.

Copyright © 2015 National Geographic Society Published by the National Geographic Society, Washington, D.C. 20036. All rights reserved. Reproduction in whole or in part without written permission of the publisher is prohibited.

Trade paperback ISBN: 978-1-4263-1959-4
Reinforced library edition ISBN: 978-1-4263-1960-0

Project Editor: Shelby Alinsky
Series Editor: Shira Evans
Art Director: Callie Broaddus
Designer: David M. Seager
Photo Editor: Lori Epstein
Editorial Assistant: Paige Towler
Design Production Assistant: Sanjida Rashid
Managing Editor: Grace Hill
Senior Production Editor: Joan Gossett
Production Manager: Lewis R. Bassford

Photo Credits
Cover, Paul Souders/The Image Bank/Getty Images; top border of pages (throughout), Rashad Ashurov/Shutterstock; 1, Corbis; 2–3, Arterra Picture Library/Alamy; 4–5, FLPA/Jules Cox/Minden Pictures; 6–7, Yva Momatiuk & John Eastcott/Minden Pictures; 8, Robert Henno/Minden Pictures; 9, Sylvain Cordier/Biosphoto; 10–11, M. Watson/ARDEA; 12–13, Pierre Vernay/Biosphoto; 14, M. Watson/ARDEA; 15, Sylvain Cordier/Biosphoto; 16–17, Paul Souders/Corbis; 18–19, Thomas Mangelsen/Minden Pictures; 20–21, Bruno Mathieu/Biosphoto; 22, Juniors Bildarchiv GmbH/Alamy; 23 (UP), irin-k/Shutterstock; 23 (CTR UP), djgis/Shutterstock; 23 (CTR LO), Michelle Marsan/Shutterstock; 23 (LO), Arve Bettum/Shutterstock; 24, Paul Souders/Corbis

National Geographic supports K–12 educators with ELA Common Core Resources. Visit natgeoed.org/commoncore for more information.

Printed in the United States of America
15/WOR/1

Answers:
In spring, the bear wakes up and eats.
In summer, the bear eats more.
In addition to berries, bugs, and grass,
it eats fish.
In fall, the bear finds a den.
In winter, the bear sleeps.